FAMILY WALKS
IN MID WALES

Laurence Main

HIGH INTEREST · LOW MILEAGE

Scarthin Books, Cromford, Derbyshire   1989

reprinted 1991, 1992

A

i

FAMILY WALKS
IN MID WALES

Family Walks Series
General Editor: Norman Taylor

THE COUNTRY CODE
Guard against all risk of fire
Fasten all gates
Keep dogs under proper control
Keep to paths across farm land
Avoid damaging fences, hedges and walls
Leave no litter
Safeguard water supplies
Protect wildlife, wild plants and trees
Go carefully along country roads
Respect the life of the countryside

Published by Scarthin Books, Cromford, Derbyshire

Phototypesetting, printing by Higham Press Ltd., Shirland, Derbyshire

ISBN 0907758 27 4

CWM EINION (ROUTE 11)

Preface

Mid Wales is superb walking country. Sandwiched between the Snowdonia National Park and the Brecon Beacons National Park, it is relatively unknown. This is one of its great assets, however, for it has scenery as magnificent as anywhere else in Wales without the crowds of tourists who cause traffic jams and make their presence felt in many other ways. Traffic jams are one thing you can escape from by becoming a pedestrian tourist and following our ancient footpaths. However crowded the beauty spot, a short walk away from its car park inevitably brings solitude. The wide, open spaces of Mid Wales bring a special sense of freedom. Wales is a different nation with its past rooted in ancient legends. Every valley has a story to tell and every place name has a meaning. It is more rewarding to gain an intimate contact with a small area than to skim across it behind the window of a car, or a bus, or train. Having sampled walking here, you will feel confined in a vehicle and will wish to know where every path you see leads.

~~~~~~~~

Acknowledgements

I would like to thank Janet Davies for the help given in reaching these walks. Thanks are also due to John Llewellyn Cooke for his special knowledge of the paths in the Llangynog area, where he erected new stiles and waymarkers. John Roberts, a local farmer, was extremely helpful with the Garthbeibio walk, while I must thank the Machynlleth M.S.C. teams who helped me erect new stiles on the Cefncoch-uchaf walk. Finally, I must thank my wife Paule and children, William, David and Chantal for testing the walks.

~~~~~~~~

About the Author

Born and educated in Oxford, Laurence Main worked as a teacher in Swindon for six years before becoming the Assistant Secretary and Education Officer of the Vegan Society in 1980. A year later, he moved to Dinas Mawddwy, in Meirionnydd, and was responsible for the bio-fuel display funded by the Vegan Society at the Centre for Alternative Technology, Machynlleth. He is now a full-time walk leader and writer of footpath guides, including 'The Dyfi Valley Way' (Bartholomew Kittiwake) and 'Walk Snowdonia and North Wales' (Bartholomew). He is also the Ramblers' Association's voluntary Footpaths Secretary for both Meirionnydd and Montgomeryshire.

CONTENTS

Location map and key to the route maps 4

Introduction 5

The Welsh Language 7

The Walks
Route 1 — *Tan-y-bwlch* 9
Route 2 — *Maesgwm* 13
Route 3 — *Pennant-Melangell* 17
Route 4 — *Llangynog* 21
Route 5 — *Plas yn Dinas* 25
Route 6 — *Meirion Mill* 29
Route 7 — *Garthbeibio* 33
Route 8 — *Abergynolwyn* 37
Route 9 — *Foel Friog* 41
Route 10 — *The Standing Stone at Cefncoch-uchaf* 45
Route 11 — *Cwm Einion* 49
Route 12 — *Penycrocbren* 53
Route 13 — *Dolforwyn Castle* 57
Route 14 — *Pen Dinas* 61
Route 15 — *Cwm Rheidol* 65
Route 16 — *Penygarreg Reservoir* 69

Appendices
— Distance of each walk from Machynlleth 74
— Routes in order of difficulty 74
— Public Transport 75
— Wet weather alternatives 75
— Tourist Information addresses 76

Location map of the walks

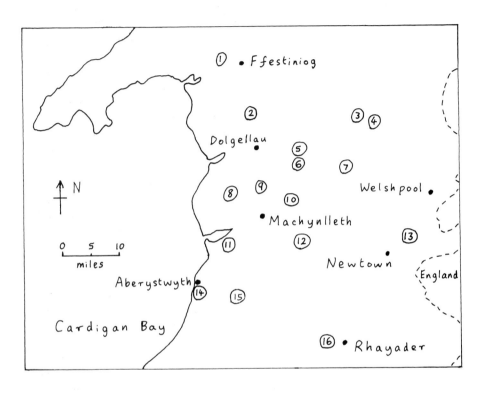

Introduction

This is a book of walks that are especially suitable for families. Hardened backpackers and experienced ramblers are catered for in other books, but here are the relatively short and undemanding walks that will be appreciated by a parent carrying a papoose or a child with young legs. Each walk has its own special feature that will attract and stimulate young minds. This may be a nature trail or woodland walk, with an emphasis on wildlife, or a riverside or lakeside stroll. The walks also encounter steam railways, mills, dams, a native Welsh castle and monuments ranging from an ancient standing stone to a memorial to the Duke of Wellington. There are also legends of Celtic saints, murders and an authentic ghost.

Walking and close contact with the real, living world is an essential part of growing up, especially in the age of television. Walking is a natural activity which requires little in the way of money and gives enjoyment without any competitive element. It is ideal for families, who do not need to join a club in order to do it. The walking season never ends, indeed each month brings its own character and invites you to repeat a walk at different times of the year. The winter is often the best time for a short, brisk walk, as long as commonsense prevails regarding the weather, precautions and clothing.

Mid Wales is a vast area. These walks are drawn from the old counties of Ceredigion (Cardiganshire), Radnorshire, Montgomeryshire and Meirionnydd (Merionethshire). They are all in the area covered by the Mid Wales region of the Wales Tourist Board. This includes the highest mountain in Britain south of the Snowdon range — Aran Fawddwy (2971 feet). There are many other mountains which add drama to the background scenery even if you don't climb them. Not even families can come to Wales without acquiring a mountain view, however, so the Garthbeibio and Penygarreg walks take you rather effortlessly to over 1000 feet, while the Penycrocbren walk takes you to over 1500 feet (but you park your car at just under 1200 feet). Mid Wales is also a land of forests and valleys, lakes and waterfalls, while its attractive coastline has cliffs, sandy beaches and wide river estuaries.

Machynlleth is an excellent base from which to explore Mid Wales. The regional headquarters of the Wales Tourist Board is housed next to the building where Owain Glyndŵr, the last independent, native prince of Wales was crowned and held a parliament. A natural route-centre, Machynlleth is served by through trains from and to London and the Midlands and is the junction for the coastal lines to Pwllheli (via Barmouth) and Aberystwyth. Traws Cambria buses also link

Machynlleth with Cardiff and Bangor, while many local bus services connect here. Alternatively, devise a route which wanders through Mid Wales, threading the walks together. A visitor from Birmingham, for instance, could start with walk 13, then go round walks 12, 16, 15, 14, 11, 10, 9, 8, 2, 1, 3, 4, 5 and 6 before finishing with walk 7.

If your children are new to rambling, it would be advisable to begin with the easiest walks, such as 2, 3, 4, 5 and 15. You could then leave strenuous walks such as 10 and 12 to the end, when they are experienced ramblers. Don't be afraid to cut a walk short, retracing your steps if necessary. This contingency particularly applies if the weather worsens or if you have under-estimated the time needed and the sun is sinking below the horizon. A pace of one mile per hour would not be unreasonable. Try to equip your child with stout shoes and a good anorak. Avoid jeans (which are very uncomfortable if soaked) and opt for several thin layers of clothing rather than one heavy jersey. A rucksack will be needed to carry spare clothes as well as your picnic, camera and maps.

It is always a good idea to carry an Ordnance Survey map and to practise using it, even if you are following a guide-book. The following Landranger sheets cover all the walks in this book: 124, 125, 135, 136 and 147. Older children may like to use a compass too, while a torch is another useful item to carry.

Refreshments are not as easily obtained in remote corners of Wales as in city parks, so be prepared. Half of the walks in this book do have a cafe, or similar, along their routes, however. Do remember that many places only open in the tourist season.

Welsh farmers are usually very friendly and tolerant towards walkers. Part of the pleasure of a walk in Mid Wales is to talk to a farmer in his field and to learn how to say a few Welsh words. The seasonal influx of English city-dwellers can bring problems, however. The Country Code must be followed, while the emphasis on sheep-farming in Wales means that dogs are not welcome in many areas. If you bring a dog on to sheep pasture you could ruin years of delicate negotiations between ramblers and farmers over access.

The Welsh Language

Welsh is a living language spoken by half a million people just a few miles away from English cities such as Liverpool, Birmingham and Bristol. There are also many Welsh-speakers living in England. Yet the Welsh language is virtually ignored on the eastern side of Offa's Dyke and schools arrange costly trips across the Channel in order to convince their pupils that other people like to speak their own languages in preference to English. In the past, English conquerors despised the Welsh language, the oldest living language in Europe, and Welsh history, with its great relevance to the ancient past of our shared island. Some knowledge of, and respect for, the language will greatly increase your enjoyment of walking in Wales.

Mid Wales is still a stronghold of the Welsh language, especially in Meirionnydd, Ceredigion and parts of Montgomeryshire. Expect to hear Welsh spoken and do try to exchange a few words in Welsh. It's also fun to translate Welsh place names into English. There are several books which can help you learn a little Welsh in a light-hearted way and a selection of them can be obtained at Tourist Information offices, bookshops and at some of the places visited on these walks (such as at Meirion Mill). Here are a few words and phrases to begin with:

Good morning — Bore da (bor-eh-da)
Good afternoon — Prynhawn da (Pre-noun-da)
Good evening — Noswaith da (Noss-wa-eeth-da)
Please — Os gwelwch yn dda (Oss-gwe-loo-kin-tha)
Thank you very much — Diolch yn fawr (Dee-olc-hen-vawr)

Aber — river-mouth, confluence	Dinas — fort, city
Afon — river	Dol, ddol — meadow
Bach, fach — small	Fawr, mawr — big
Bryn — hill	Ffynnon — well, spring
Bwlch — pass, defile	Foel, moel — rounded hill
Cae — field	Llan — church
Caer — fort	Llyn — lake
Carreg — rock	Nant — brook, stream
Cefn — ridge	Pen — top, head
Coch — red	Plas — mansion
Coed — woodland	Pont, bont — bridge
Cwm — cirque, valley	Ucha, uchaf — upper

Symbols used on the route maps

The footpath route
with direction from
the start

(4) etc — Number corresponding
with route directions

..... Other paths (not always
rights of way)

Railway

Motor road

River or stream
with driection of flow

Hedge or fence

Canal

Wall

Bridge

Standing stone or monument

Trees

G — Gate

Buildings

S — Stile

Ruin

P — Signpost

+ Church or chapel

Viewpoint

X Campsite

Earthworks

↑ N Direction of north
(not always at the top
of the page)

O S — Relevant Ordnance Survey
Landranger map sheet

Each map has a scale in miles and a gradient profile showing the height in feet above sea
level and the distance in miles from the start of the walk.

Tan-y-bwlch

Outline   Tan-y-bwlch Station ~ Nature Trail ~ Lakeside Road ~ Forest Walk ~ Lakeside Road ~ Nature Trail ~ Tan-y-bwlch Station.

Summary   A woodland path leads down from the Ffestiniog Railway's station at Tan-y-bwlch to a lakeside road. This leads to more paths through woodland, climbing back up to and above the Ffestiniog Railway to enjoy splendid views over the Vale of Ffestiniog and the Dwyryd estuary. The Plas, or mansion, is passed on the return walk.

Attractions   This walk combines well with a trip on the Ffestiniog Railway. This independent narrow-gauge line provides a useful service by linking British Rail's Cambrian Coast line at Minffordd (the two lines cross here, the Ffestiniog Railway has a terminus at Porthmadog, but this is nearly a mile from the town's British Rail Station) with the Conwy Valley line at Blaenau Ffestiniog. The station at the start of this walk, Tan-y-bwlch, was opened in 1873, closed in 1939 and re-opened in 1958. It was the upper terminus of the railway until 1968. The walk crosses the line at Plas Halt, which was opened in 1963. This replaced an old private halt which stood where the walk recrosses the railway and was used by the Oakeley family when they lived in the Plas.

     Plas Tan-y-bwlch is now the Snowdonia National Park Residential Study Centre, which offers a variety of interesting courses. It was formerly the home of the Oakeley family, who owned and promoted the slate quarries in Blaenau Ffestiniog. The Ffestiniog Railway was built in 1836 to carry slate to Porthmadog (downhill by gravity, with horses pulling the empty trucks uphill). The Oakeleys enjoyed the life of the landed gentry and were responsible for stocking their gardens with many exotic plants, including the rhododendrons. After the death of the last member of the family, in 1961, an attempt was made to turn the Estate into a country club (hence the chalets) before it was bought jointly by the Countryside Commission and the National Park Committee in 1969.

     Most of the trees are native deciduous species, which encourage a wide variety of wildlife to live here. Look out for woodpeckers, grey squirrels and the 300 different insects associated with the oak tree. A fenced enclosure on your left as you walk down the nature trail at the start, displays (and protects) a labelled selection of young trees.

Refreshments   There is a refreshments room in the ticket office at Tan-y-bwlch Station (and a miniature railway nearby).

Route 1

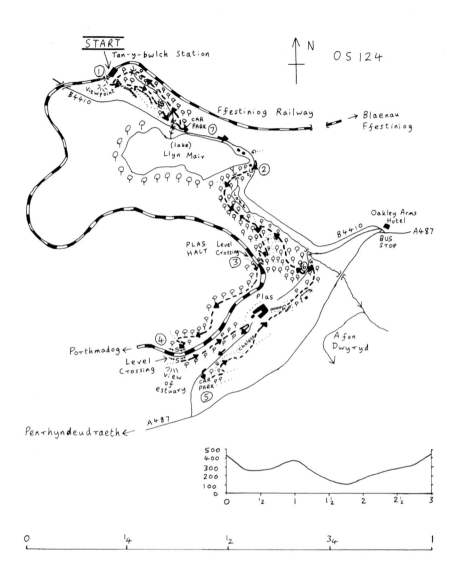

Route 1
Tan-y-bwlch

3 miles

START   *Tan-y-bwlch is a station on the Ffestiniog Railway about half-way along its 14 mile route between Porthmadog and Blaenau Ffestiniog. It is highly recommended that you arrive by train. You could drive to the station car park, however, which is just off the B4410 about a mile from its junction with the A487 at the Oakley Arms Hotel, and take a return trip on the train from here after this walk. The train service is seasonal, so if you rely on public transport in the winter, take a bus to the Oakley Arms, Maentwrog. There are also car parks along the walk, as marked on the map. (G.R. SH650415)*

ROUTE

1. *Cross the footbridge over the Ffestiniog Railway from its island platform at Tan-y-bwlch, going left to pass the refreshments on your right. Divert right to the viewpoint, return to the path and fork right, with the wall on your left. Follow this path down to a car park, crossing a footbridge on the way. Turn left along the road with the lake on your right. Continue to a gate and stile on the right at the end of the lake.*

2. *Go over the stile and follow the track through the trees, passing a small lake (the old mill pond) to your left. Fork right, uphill, at a path junction and zigzag up to a gate which gives access to the railway at the Plas Halt. Cross the line carefully to the gate opposite.*

3. *Turn left to follow the path overlooking the railway and the valley on your left. Zigzag downhill to a stile in the railway fence.*

4. *Cross the railway carefully to a stile opposite. This was where the Oakeley family halt was. Follow the path down to the Plas on your left. Turn sharply right along the drive to reach the car park.*

5. *Turn sharply left through the car park to follow the woodland path which is waymarked with yellow, red and blue arrows, forking left just after the chalets to walk across the grass in front of the Plas and past a pond on your right to a gate ahead. Follow the blue and yellow arrows along a path to a gate leading to the drive. Turn left along the drive, looking for a woodland path on your right.*

6. *Turn right along the woodland path back to the lakeside road.*

7. *Back at the lakeside car park, turn right up the waymarked nature trail, with the stream on your left, back to Tan-y-bwlch Station.*

Public Transport   The Ffestiniog Railway would have earned the title of 'a really useful railway' from the Rev. W. Awdry. Other narrow gauge steam trains in Wales are pleasant spurs, or even isolated stretches of track. The Ffestiniog helps to form a vital through route, however. You can buy through tickets from British Rail stations at Llandudno or Barmouth, or even a day circular tour ticket via Llandudno Junction, Chester, Shrewsbury and Barmouth. Trains run from March to October and over Christmas (tel. Porthmadog 512340). The nearest bus stop is the Oakeley Arms, Maentwrog (bus no.'s 1, 1B, 35 & 38 — regular and frequent services from Blaenau Ffestiniog).

THE START OF THE RIVERSIDE PATH AT MAESGWM

12

Maesgwm

Outline   Picnic Place ~ Forest Trail ~ Maesgwm Visitor Centre ~ Picnic Place.

Summary   A gentle woodland walk alongside the river Eden is followed by a stroll through a woodland glade to the Maesgwm Visitor Centre.

Attractions   Maesgwm Visitor Centre provides an introduction to the Coed y Brenin. This is the Welsh for King's Forest. There was an oak forest here in the days of Cadwgan, prince of Powys in 1100. When the Vaughan family of Nannau sold the land to the Forestry Commission in 1922, it was largely replanted with conifers. The forest received its royal name in 1935, to commemorate the silver jubilee of King George V.

Coed y Brenin is a fine example of the way that the Forestry Commission has catered for the public by waymarking forest tracks and producing maps and guides. The Visitor Centre at Maesgwn interprets the environment in an attractive way, with models and displays. An audio-visual show is usually available, while a shop sells souvenirs and a wooden sign workshop can also be visited.

The area has a wealth of interest. Drovers used to gather at Dol-gefeiliau to have their cattle shod before the trek to England. Gold mining is a major part of the local heritage and is still carried on. Forestry is the chief employer now, however, with tourism also important to the local economy.

The walk is up the beautiful valley of the river Eden, with its rushing waters. The retention of oaks and birches makes the riverside more attractive, while as the walk turns to head back to the start, your way is through a fine grove of beech trees that must have been planted in the 17th century. Amongst the wildlife of the forest is the fallow deer, while the forest glades are noted for their wild flowers and woodland butterflies.

Refreshments   Refreshments are available at the Maesgwm Visitor Centre.

Route 2

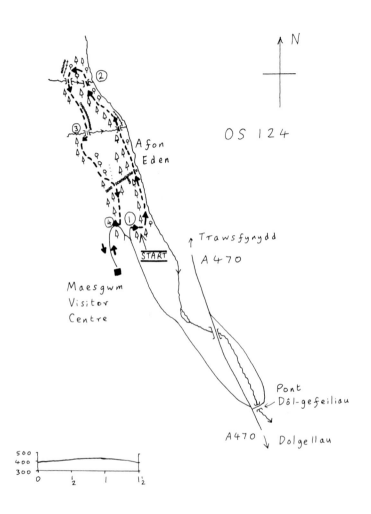

N

OS 124

Afon
Eden

Trawsfynydd

A470

START

Maesgwm
Visitor
Centre

Pont
Dôl-gefeiliau

A470 ↓ Dolgellau

500
400
300

0   ½   1   1½

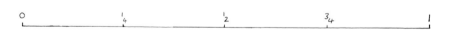

0   ¼   ½   ¾   1

14

Route 2

Maesgwm

1½ miles

START *Maesgwm Visitor Centre is signposted off the A470, on your left, as you come from Dolgellau. The turning is about two miles north of Ganllwyd. Park at the picnic place. (G.R. SH716277)*

ROUTE

1. *Start near the entrance of the picnic place car park. Walk to the bank of the river Eden and turn left, walking upstream with the river on your right. The path is waymarked with white-topped posts.*

2. *After crossing the second footbridge over a tributary of the Eden, bear left with the path through a grove of beech trees, making a semi-circle to re-cross the stream higher up by another footbridge. Go ahead to walk with a wall on your left.*

3. *Cross a little footbridge and follow a narrow path around a forest glade and on past the picnic place on your left.*

4. *Go right up the road to the Maesgwm Visitor Centre, then retrace your steps to the car park at the picnic place.*

Public Transport Gwynedd bus No. 35 (between Machynlleth and Blaenau Ffestiniog) passes the turning off the A470 which is signposted to the Maesgwm Visitor Centre. Ask for Pont Dol-gefeiliau. There is a fairly frequent weekday service. Consult the current bus timetable leaflet for Meirionnydd produced by Gwynedd County Council, or telephone Caernarfon 4121.

BISTORT   Pale pink. June - Oct.

THE PATH GOING EAST FROM ST. MELANGELL'S CHURCH.

Pennant-Melangell

Outline St. Melangell's Church ~ Llechwedd-y-garth ~ Pontbren Fain ~ St. Melangell's Church.

Summary A gentle stroll in Cwm Pennant, the valley made famous by the saint whose church stands at the start of this walk. Clear field paths are followed to Llechwedd-y-garth, from where a track leads down to the lane which leads to the church.

Attractions In the late 6th century, an Irish princess called Melangell (or Monacella in Latin) was expected to marry a young man from a leading Irish family. The marriage was arranged by the king, her father. Melangell had no choice in the matter and did not want to marry the one chosen for her. She would bring shame on her family if she refused the young man, however. Unable to deny her true feelings, she fled well away from her father's influence, like a hunted animal. Committing herself to the mercy of the waves, she floated in a coracle to Wales, where she discovered this secluded valley and made it her home.

Untroubled for 14 years, Melangell established a harmonious relationship with the creatures that shared her remote valley. Then, in 604, the peace was shattered by a rough intruder. Brochfael Ysgithrog (Brochfael of the Tusks), the prince of Powys, came upon Cwm Pennant whilst out hunting. Excited by the abundance of wildlife in this valley, the prince's hunting-dogs excitedly sniffed a variety of scents before settling on a hare which was spotted trying to escape up the valley.

The hare fled in terror to Melangell, hiding under her dress. The huntsmen wondered why the dogs had suddenly stopped the chase when they followed them to a small clearing where the dogs were still, staring at a beautiful young woman. Without any sign of fear, Melangell quietly faced them, guarding the hare. Brochfael tried to impose his authority by ordering the young woman out of the way and the dogs to kill their prey. There was not the slightest movement and the little woman maintained a dignified bearing. Brochfael respected her courage and asked who she was. After hearing her story, the prince was so impressed that he gave the saint land to build a nunnery. Hares were thereafter protected in this district and to call after a hunted hare 'God and Melangell go with thee' should save it from pursuing hounds.

Refreshments There are no shops or cafes here, but Llangynog, from where Route 4 starts, is just over two miles away and has both a shop and a cafe.

Route 3

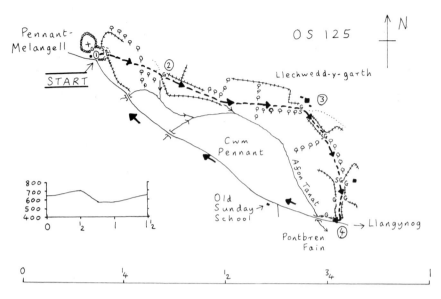

Pennant-Melangell

OS 125

↑ N

START

Llechwedd-y-garth

① ② ③

Cwm Pennant

Afon Tanat

800
700
600
500
400

0   ¼   ½   ¾   1

Old Sunday School

Pontbren Fain

④ → Llangynog

0   ¼   ½   ¾   1

ST. MELANGELL'S CHURCH

18

Route 3

Pennant-Melangell
1½ miles

START *Park your car near St. Melangell's church at Pennant-Melangell. This is near the end of a quiet lane up Cwm Pennant, two miles west of Llangynog, which is on the B4391 between Bala and Llanfyllin. (G.R. SJ024265)*

ROUTE

1. *With the church at your back, walk with a wall on your left towards a field gate. Turn left over a stile to avoid opening the gate and turn right immediately, to follow the clear path across the field ahead from the gate. Ignore a track going uphill on your left.*

2. *Go ahead over a waymarked stile beside a gate and continue with the fence on your left. Veer slightly left uphill when you are near a bend in the river below on your right. Walk with trees on your right until the buildings of Llechwedd-y-garth.*

3. *Having crossed another waymarked stile beside a gate, keeping the buildings on your left, bear right down a fenced track to another waymarked stile beside a gate. Continue downhill along this track to reach a lane near a letter box.*

4. *Turn right along this lane. Ignore a turning on your left. Continue past the old Sunday School and over two bridges back to the start.*

Public Transport   There is no public transport to this remote valley.

MOUNTAIN PANSY   Yellow/purple. May - Aug.

LOOKING SOUTH ACROSS THE TANAT VALLEY

Llangynog

Outline   Llangynog ~ Afon Tanat ~ Dismantled Railway ~ Llangynog.

Summary   A very easy, flat, riverside path in the beautiful Tanat Valley leads to the trackbed of the old Tanat Valley Light Railway. Your return to Llangynog is along a quiet lane at the foot of Craig Rhiwarth.

Attractions   The Romans may have mined lead at Llangynog. The Ancient Britons certainly lived in a hillfort on top of Craig Rhiwarth. This is a spectacular site, overlooking the Tanat Valley and the moorland of the Berwyns. Over 150 small round huts were sited on its sunny southern terraces and the place was noted for fairies.

Llangynog is named after Saint Cynog, the illegitimate and eldest son of Brychan, who founded the dynasty of Brycheiniog in South Wales in the late fifth century. The mountain range that borders the village is named after his brother Berwyn. The place became famous in the 18th century, however, when its lead mines were at their peak. Pure galena from Llangynog netted the owners of Powis Castle £20,000 per annum. The lead was exhausted by 1877, but the slate quarries were established by then as well. The slates were brought down the steep slope in sledges containing about five hundredweight each. Conductors sat on top of the loaded sledges to steer them down the slope with their feet. If they couldn't brake with their feet on the ground, they might have to jump clear as the sledge and its slates crashed down a precipice.

The cultural life of the community was rich, with a noted choir and harpists, including the famous Thomas Lloyd. The outside world intruded, however, when a railway was at last built to Llangynog. There had been a scheme in 1860 for a through route from the West Midlands to the Cambrian Coast via Llangynog, but the prospect of tunnelling under the Berwyns and the opposition of the Earl of Powis meant that Llangynog eventually became the terminus of the Tanat Valley Light Railway in 1904 (officially, trains may have run unofficially in 1903). This standard gauge railway started at Blodwell Junction, stemming from Oswestry. It revived the slate quarries but this trade ceased in 1939 and the upper section of line beyond Llanrhaiadr Mochnant was closed in 1953 (with passenger services on the whole line ceasing in 1951). The remaining section was closed in 1960 after flood damage.

Refreshments   There is a cafe and a shop near the car park.

Route 4

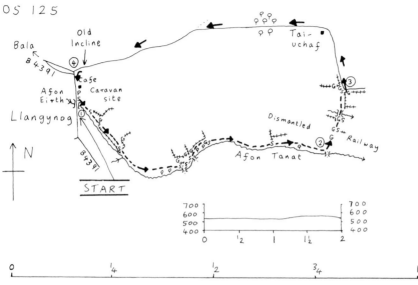

OS 125

Bala
B4391
Afon Eirth
Llangynog

↑ N

Old Incline

④

Cafe
Caravan site
P
①

B4391

START

Tai-uchaf

③

Dismantled

Afon Tanat

②

Railway

700
600
500
400

700
600
500
400

0   ½   1   1½   2

0   ¼   ½   ¾   1

JOHN LLEWELLYN COOKE WITH ONE OF THE STILES HE ERECTED ON THE
LLANGYNOG WALK

22

Route 4

Llangynog

2 miles

START   *Look for a car park opposite the shop and on your right as you go through Llangynog along the B4391 towards Bala. There are public toilets, and an information board for visitors is planned. (G.R. SJ054262)*

ROUTE

1. *Turn right from the car park and cross the bridge over the river Eirth. Turn right immediately after the bridge and before the cafe to cross a stile and follow the signposted footpath along the river bank. Keep the river on your right (it joins the river Tanat after 400 yards) and follow the waymarked path over stiles. Continue as far as the third footbridge, but do not cross it.*

2. *Instead turn left, away from the river. Go through an isolated gate to cross the bed of the old Tanat Valley Light Railway. Go ahead over a stile beside a gate and continue over another stile beside a gate to cross a stream. Walk with a fence on your right to a stile beside a gate which gives access to a lane on your right.*

3. *Bear left along this quiet lane, which bends left to lead back to Llangynog, passing an old incline on your right.*

4. *Turn left to pass the cafe on your left. Cross the bridge over the river Eirth again to reach the car park on your left.*

Public Transport   Unfortunately, there is none as the railway is no longer with us.

TURN RIGHT OVER THE STILE JUST AFTER THE BRIDGE OVER THE RIVER EIRTH.

23

THE PATH ABOVE THE CARAVAN SITE, NEAR THE END OF ROUTE 5.

Plas yn Dinas

Outline Plas yn Dinas ~ Dolhir Lodge ~ Cerist Bridge ~ Old Road ~ Pont Dol-y-bont ~ Gwesty'r Llew Coch ~ Plas yn Dinas.

Summary A fairly level walk along both sides of the Cerist Valley, a tributary of the river Dyfi, can be enjoyed at any season, but puff-balls and other mushrooms can be found in the autumn. The scenery is superb, while you may see a ghost along the way.

Attractions The swings are at the start of this walk, on the site of the old Plas, or mansion, at Dinas Mawddwy. If this creates a problem at the start, you can entice the children away with the prospect of seeing a ghost. The swings will still be there at the end. The old Plas was destroyed by a fire in 1917, but the Buckley family that had built the noble mansion in 1864 for £70,000 (£700,000 in today's prices) hadn't lived in it since 1900. It took three years to construct and the family, who had made their fortune in business in Manchester, invested unwisely in Welsh estates and went bankrupt.

The ghost is at Dolhir Lodge, the building near the A470 road when you emerge from the grounds of the old Plas. There are numerous tales of this particular haunted house. It used to be a guest house and it was not uncommon for guests to book for a whole week, only to leave in a hurry after the first night. Ghostly hands would pull the blankets off the beds during the night and the rooms would go suddenly cold.

Refreshments There is a shop in Dinas Mawddwy, while the Coffee Shop in the old station is half a mile to the south (see the Meirion Mill walk, Route 6).

GREAT TIT

Yellow, grey, black. 14cm.

25

Route 5

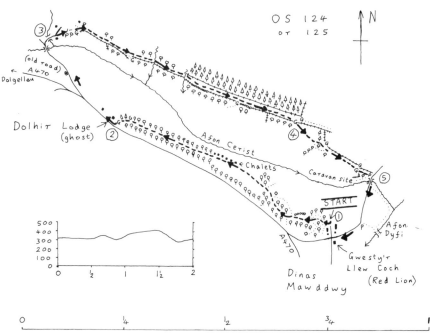

THE VIEW ACROSS THE DYFI VALLEY FROM DINAS MAWDDWY

26

Route 5
Plas yn Dinas

2 miles

START   *The grounds of the old Plas at Dinas Mawddwy now house a small council housing estate — hence the swings and the parking space. Go to Dinas Mawddwy (on the A470 one mile north of its junction with the A458 at Mallwyd) and take the access road at the head of the main street of the village, opposite the 'Gwesty'r Llew Coch' (Red Lion). The swings are near the parking spaces. (G.R. SH858150)*

ROUTE

1. *With your back to the 'flying saucer' of the swings, walk south. Go right along the track into the woodland just before the bungalows. Fork right immediately, however, leaving the main track which goes to the old stables. Go ahead past a wall on your right to a track which you follow round on your left. Stick to this track, passing chalets on your right, to the road at Dolhir Lodge (where the ghost is).*

2. *Turn right along the A470, which has a wide, grassy verge. Bear right down a lane which used to be the main road to Dolgellau. The old road can be seen through a gate on your left as you descend to cross the river Cerist by a bridge. Fork right to cross a second bridge.*

3. *Climb up the lane, forking right, then going ahead along the old cart road which bears right to run along the side of the 1709 ft. Foel Benddin and above the river Cerist on your right.*

4. *At the end of a conifer plantation on your left, turn right through a gate, then half-left to follow a path downhill, through trees and beside a hedge on your left to a gate ahead, above a caravan site on your right. Go ahead to reach a road at a public footpath signpost.*

5. *Turn right along the road, crossing the bridge over the river Cerist and climbing back to Dinas Mawddwy. When you reach the crossroads at the 'Gwesty'r Llew Coch', turn right back to the swings in the Plas.*

Public Transport   There are infrequent bus services to Dinas Mawddwy from Machynlleth (S18) and Dolgellau (27). Consult the current bus timetable leaflet for Meirionnydd produced by Gwynedd County Council, or telephone Caernarfon 4121.

THE VIEW ACROSS THE DYFI VALLEY TO DINAS MAWDDWY FROM THE
OLD CART TRACK.

Meirion Mill

Outline Meirion Mill ~ Pont Minllyn ~ Cambrian Way ~ Coed Cefncoch ~ Dyfi Valley Way ~ Pont Minllyn ~ Meirion Mill.

Summary A peaceful valley path is left for a delightful, waymarked, path up through broad-leaved trees to an old cart-track at the edge of a conifer forest. This gives fine views across the valley of the river Dyfi as you turn back to the start. A gradual descent is made over sheep pasture, past an old ruined cottage and over ladder-stiles, back to the old bridge over the Dyfi and the Meirion Mill.

Attractions One of the most beautiful valleys in Wales provides the setting for this walk, near Dinas Mawddwy. The start and finish is at the Meirion Mill, where there is so much to see and do that it is better to do the walk first or you may never fit it in. An old road bridge, now closed to motor traffic, takes you across the swiftly-flowing river Dyfi. This is the middle of three bridges, so it is hard not to look over the parapet on both sides. Upstream is the modern road bridge while downstream is the pack-horse bridge built in the 17th century. Long before that, a Roman road crossed the river here.

The valley path follows the route of Tony Drake's 'Cambrian Way', here 186 miles from its start in Cardiff and with 88 miles still to go to its northern terminus at Conwy. This is sheep-farming country, but you may see a herd of beef cattle down in the meadow on your left before you turn up along the woodland path to an old cart-track. This forms part of another long-distance route, the 'Dyfi Valley Way'. The views from the valley path are good, but the extra height makes them even better on your return journey. Sweeping from left to right, you can see the valley of the Dyfi, now starting to meander gracefully, the village of Dinas Mawddwy across the valley with the 1568 ft. high Foel Dinas behind it, the valley of the Cerist, a tributary of the Dyfi, and the steep slopes of the 1709 ft. Foel Benddin.

The old ruined cottage which you pass on your descent back to the start is interesting because local people can still recall when a huge family (at least twenty children) were somehow shoe-horned into it. Nor were they little people, as one was a famed village blacksmith. This eastern side of the valley is particularly favoured on a late afternoon or early evening, when it enjoys the sun while the other side of the valley is in shadow.

continued on page 32

29

Route 6

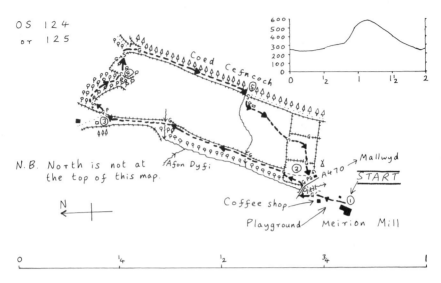

OS 124
or 125

Coed Cefncoch

N.B. North is not at the top of this map.

Afon Dyfi

Mallwyd

A470

START

Coffee shop

Playground

Meirion Mill

N

0   ¼   ½   ¾   1

THE MEIRION MILL.

30

Route 6

Meirion Mill   2 miles

START   *Meirion Mill is on the A470 one mile north of its junction with the A458 at Mallwyd, about eleven miles east of Dolgellau. (G.R. SH859139)*

ROUTE

1. *Walk back from the car park at the Meirion Mill towards the Old Station Coffee Shop, opposite which are steps leading down to the riverbank for a view of the old pack-horse bridge. Climb back up the steps to turn right and go through the old station gates. Cross the river Dyfi by the old road bridge on your right and cross the A470 carefully to a signposted kissing-gate at the entrance to Celyn Brithion campsite.*

2. *Follow the valley track past caravans to a gate ahead. Continue with the river Dyfi down on your left and a fence on your right. You come to some trees where the track crosses an attractive little stream and your way is now fenced until a gate on your right, with a public footpath signpost beside it. This is just before a ruin down on your left and Tan-y-bwlch farmhouse ahead.*

3. *Turn right uphill through the signposted gate and turn left immediately to reach a stile. Cross this to enter some attractive woodland. The waymarked path turns right up through the trees until you reach a stile in the top fence.*

4. *Veer left after this stile through a line of trees to cross the fence on your left by a stile just above a gate. Turn right after crossing this stile to walk with the fence on your right to a path junction. Bear right, through a gate, along the old cart-track. There are conifer trees going up the hillside on your left, while the fence and the view is on your right.*

5. *Turn right across a ladder-stile, just after a stream crosses your path. Go ahead to an old ruined cottage and bear left downhill to reach another ladder-stile in the fence ahead. Go ahead until you are level with a gate in the fence on your left. Turn right downhill to go through a gate and cross the small caravan site back to the signposted gate beside the A470. Return carefully across this main road to cross the river Dyfi by the old road bridge and to re-enter Meirion Mill.*

Public Transport   Buses are infrequent but they will drop you right at the Meirion Mill. Current times must be checked, but at the time of writing there are buses from Machynlleth (S18) every Wednesday and

Back at the Meirion Mill, you can walk where trains once ran beside the platform of Dinas Mawddwy Station, now a highly-recommended Coffee Shop which serves wholefood meals. The last train to run on this line was on 5th September, 1950. It was a goods train as passenger services were withdrawn in 1930, with the exception of the local Sunday Schools' annual outing to Aberystwyth. The old station yard now houses Meirion Mill, a working woollen mill where you can see the weaving of traditional Welsh fabrics in exciting modern colours and styles. The Mill is open to visitors all year from Mondays to Fridays, while its shop remains open at weekends during the summer. Between the Mill and the Old Station Coffee Shop is an excellent children's playground.

Refreshments The Old Station Coffee Shop can provide drinks, snacks and meals. Drinks are also available in the Meirion Mill.

Saturday and from Dolgellau (27) every Tuesday and Friday and on Thursdays in the summer. These services allow several hours between buses.

THE VIEW ACROSS THE VALLEY OF THE AFON BANWY FROM
GARTHBEIBIO CHURCHYARD.

32

Garthbeibio

Outline   Garthbeibio Church ~ Moorland Tracks ~ Hollow Oak ~
Foel-lwyd ~ Garthbeibio Church ~ Roman Road.

Summary   Good, clear tracks and farm access lanes provide a pleasant
introduction to the moorlands of Mid Wales for people driving into Wales
along the A458 from Welshpool. The views are extensive, taking in the
valley of the Afon Banwy, the peaks of the Arans and the oak-clad slopes
of Cwm Twrch.

Attractions   The fresh air and scenery are enough to give you an excuse
to stop the car and, perhaps, take your first walk in Wales. The colours of
the leaves in autumn, and this walk's proximity to England (Offa's Dyke
is less than 20 miles down the A458) also make it ideal for a day-trip in
October or November. The route goes slightly higher than 1000 feet, but
the tracks are never strenuous and you do start from a height of 600 feet.
    Garthbeibio church is dedicated to its founder, St. Tydecho, who
came here from Brittany in the 6th century. A brother of St. Samson, and
a first cousin to St. Cadfan, St. Tydecho was also a nephew of King
Arthur. Tydecho was the son of Amwn Ddu, who married Anna, a
daughter of Meurig ab Twedrig and a sister of King Arthur, whose
territory was the modern Glamorgan, Gwent and parts of
Gloucestershire, Avon and Somerset. Garthbeibio church stands high
above the modern road, but was probably beside the old Roman road
which linked Wroxeter with Brithdir.
    Among the graves in Garthbeibio churchyard is one for John Evans
and his wife, who were murdered at their home, Foel-lwyd, in 1905. They
had been drinking at Ty'n-y-llan (now a house, then a pub.), opposite
Garthbeibio church with Roland Llywarch, a native of these parts who
had worked in London and was a butcher by trade. Their butchered
bodies were found the next morning and Roland Llywarch was caught
three days later at Llanfyllin. The butcher is reputed to have washed his
bloody hands in the well opposite the hollow oak near Foel-lwyd. The
harpist, Evan Evans (bardic name 'Telynor-y-Waen-Oer') is also buried
here.

Refreshments   Garthbeibio has gone dry, losing both its holy well and its
pub (but then you don't want to be butchered, do you?). If you are
desperate, there is a shop on the roadside in Foel.

Route 7

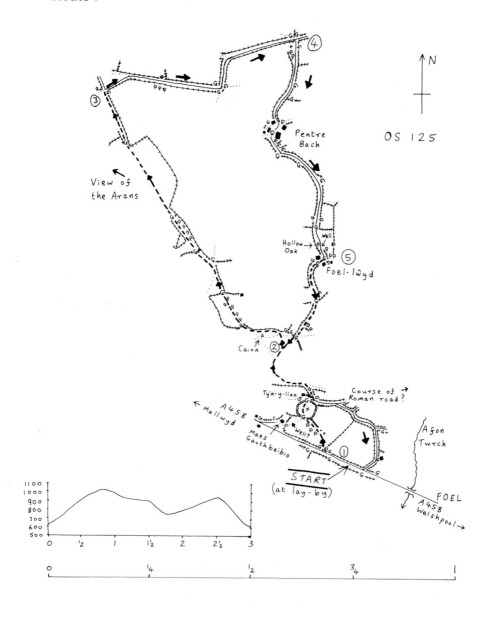

N

OS 125

④

③

View of
the Arans

Pentre
Bach

Well

Hollow→
Oak

⑤
Foel-lŵyd

Cairn ②

Tŷ'n-y-llan

Course of →
Roman road?

← A458
Mallwyd

Well?

Maes
Garthbeibio

Afon
Twrch

①

START
(at lay-by)

FOEL

A458
Welshpool→

1100
1000
900
800
700
600
500

0   ½   1   1½   2   2½   3

0   ¼   ½   ¾   1

34

Route 7
Garthbeibio

3 miles

START   *Look for a lay-by on your right as you drive westwards along the A458 from Foel, which is between Llanfair Caereinion and Mallwyd. Cross the bridge over the river west of Foel and look for a lane 200 yards after it, on your right. The lay-by is just after the lane. (G.R. SH987117).*

ROUTE

1. *Walk west from the lay-by (towards Mallwyd) and go through the second gate on your right. Bear left uphill between the trees and an old broken wall, to reach a small gate which leads into the churchyard of St. Tydecho's church. Before going through it, however, divert downhill on your left to look for a damp depression in the ground which could mark the spot of either St. Tydecho's Well, which was famous for curing rheumatism, or of another holy well which was near it and was called Ffynnon Rhigos (and cured sore eyes). Climb back to the churchyard and walk through it, passing the church on your right, to reach a gate leading to a lane. Go right for a few yards, then left up a track. Stick to this clear track as you climb. Notice a cairn on your left and go towards it, with a fence on your right.*

2. *Follow the obvious track, going through a gate to cross a field to a second gate. Ignore a gate in the fence on your right but keep to the track through a gate ahead to pass trees on your right and a fence on your left. Maintain your direction after going through another gate, but notice the Arans away on your left. Go straight on to a gate ahead to continue with a fence on your right to reach a lane.*

3. *Turn right along this lane. Bend left downhill with it, but turn right at a junction by an old chapel.*

4. *Pass the old chapel on your right and follow this lane through the farmyard of Pentre Bach to a second farmyard, Foel-lwyd, where the gruesome murder took place. Just before this farm, however, notice the hollow oak tree on the right of the lane opposite the old well.*

5. *Go through the gate after Foel-lwyd to follow the track which leads past a ruin on your left back to your outward track. Return to Garthbeibio church, but keep left this time, along what may have been the old Roman road, to follow the lane downhill and round to your right back to the lay-by.*

Public Transport As we go to press, there is news of a new bus (127) between Oswestry and Aberystwyth on every Friday in the summer (monthly in the winter). Tel. Llansilin 383 for full details.

A SERIES OF MINIATURE WATERFALLS ON NANT GWERNOL

Route 8

Abergynolwyn

Outline Slate Quarry Village ~ Forest Walk ~ Talyllyn Railway.

Summary A moderately strenuous walk up and down the valley of the Nant Gwernol. Fairly level forest paths are followed until an access road leads across the Talyllyn Railway and down to Abergynolwyn.

Attractions The chief feature of this walk is the Talyllyn Railway. Its terminus at Nant Gwernol Station is passed twice, so it would be easy to adapt the route to suit one, or even two, walks from this station, as indicated in the route description. The Talyllyn is one of the most romantic 'Great Little Trains of Wales'. Readers of the Rev. W. Awdry's railway books will find it familiar, indeed 'Peter Sam' and other engines from the Skarloey Railway have been known to make guest appearances on the Talyllyn. Even if you don't arrive at Nant Gwernol by train, do carry a Talyllyn Railway timetable, so that you can be at the level crossing when a train approaches (but DO TAKE CARE WHEN CROSSING THE RAILWAY). Trains run on this track from Easter until October and over Christmas (tel. Tywyn 710472). The line runs for 7¼ miles from Tywyn and was first opened to passenger traffic in 1867, a year after it was opened to carry slates from the quarries at Abergynolwyn to Tywyn, for transhipment to the main line railway. It achieved fame when Sir Henry Haydn Jones, the last individual owner, helped volunteers to form the Talyllyn Railway Preservation Society to save the line from closure in 1950, thus setting a precedent.

This is a picturesque walk in its own right. Nant Gwernol means Stream of the Alders and the woodland walk passes a series of little waterfalls. The outward section of the forest walk is through the native sessile oak wood, while the return route is through conifer plantations. Look out for the Alltwyllt Incline, above the Nant Gwernol Station. Horse-drawn trams used to bring slate from higher up the valley to the head of this incline, where they were lowered to the steam-hauled railway by gravity. The ruin of the old windinghouse can still be seen. Abergynolwyn (Aber means the mouth of a river, while olwyn means white wheel, or whirlpool — there used to be a whirlpool where the Afon Dysynni met Nant Gwernol) was built in the 1860s to serve the Bryn Eglwys Slate Quarry. A small museum stands near the school.

Refreshments Hilary's Kitchen is an excellent wholefood cafe near the start of this walk. You can also buy ice-creams from the shop on the roadside near the car park, opposite the Railway Inn.

Route 8

WATCH OUT FOR TRAINS AT THE LEVEL CROSSING!

Route 8

Abergynolwyn

2¾ miles

START *Abergynolwyn is on the B4405 about 7 miles north-east of Tywyn and 5 miles south-west of its junction with the A487 at Minffordd. A car park is in the centre of the village, on your right if coming from Tywyn. (G.R. SH678069)*

ROUTE

1. *From the car park, walk along the lane away from the main road, passing Hilary's Kitchen on your right. Climb up the steep road until a sign on your right points to a path leading to 'Gorsaf Nant Gwernol Station' (this is a bilingual sign, gorsaf being the Welsh for station and preceding the name).*

2. *Turn right along this path. Cross a stile on your left to follow a charming woodland path, with the stream (Nant Gwernol) on your right. Pass a footbridge, which leads to Nant Gwernol Station, on your right. IF YOU ARRIVE HERE BY TRAIN, you can start the walk from this footbridge.*

3. *Continue walking upstream, with Nant Gwernol on your right. You cross a footbridge to enter oak forest. Keep ahead over a stile and step across a tribuatry stream before coming to a footbridge on your right. Use this to cross Nant Gwernol.*

4. *After crossing the footbridge, follow the level path on your right. Remains of an old truck indicate that this was once a tramway. You will eventually reach a ruin on your right, the winding-house of the Alltwyllt Incline.*

5. *Do not go down the incline, unless you want to return to Nant Gwernol Station. IF YOU ARRIVE AT NANT GWERNOL BY TRAIN, this is another place where you could start this walk. Ignoring the narrow path which climbs into the trees on your left, go ahead along the path which overlooks Nant Gwernol on your right. Keep to this path as it broadens into a forest track and curves to the left. Look out for an access road bending downhill on your right.*

6. *Follow the access road downhill on your right. Cross the railway with great care and continue to the B4405. Go right along this road back to Abergynolwyn, passing a playground with swings on your left.*

Public Transport   It would be unthinkable to come here and not enjoy a ride on the Talyllyn Railway. If you come out of season, however, you can still reach Abergynolwyn by public transport. There is a regular bus service (No. 30) between Tywyn and Minffordd via Abergynolwyn. The bus stop is at the Railway Inn, opposite the car park. Meirionydd bus timetable leaflets are available from the County Planning Department, County Council Offices, Caernarfon, Gwynedd, LL55 1SH (send a 9" x 6" s.a.e.).

FOLLOW THE WHITE FOOTPRINTS ALONG THE FOEL FRIOG FOREST TRAIL

Route 9

Foel Friog

Outline   Picnic Place ~ Forest Trail ~ Picnic Place.

Summary   This is a waymarked forest trail close to the village of Corris. White topped posts and white footprint waymarks make navigation easy, but there is a moderately strenuous climb up to a viewpoint, where there is a superb view of Cadair Idris. The best part of this fine walk is where a narrow path winds down through native deciduous trees.

Attractions   Foel Friog is an excellent forest trail. Its best feature is the sessile oak forest which you reach after the viewpoint. These native deciduous trees provide habitats for a variety of wildlife. Sessile oak forest is the natural climax vegetation of nearly all of Wales, yet it is now almost extinct. Man the exploiter has cleared the trees in order to graze sheep and to plant faster-growing alien conifers. There is a lot to be said for learning to live in harmony with the natural environment, however. A visit to the nearby Centre for Alternative Technology will allow you the chance to see a display of bio-fuel, showing how our native deciduous trees could be replanted as safe, renewable and storeable energy forests.,

The views from this walk include Aberllefenni, where slate is still quarried. The slate industry in the Corris area was thriving in the 19th and early 20th centuries. As a result, a railway was built from the quarries at Aberllefenni down the Dulas Valley via Corris to Machynlleth. This 2 ft. 3 ins. gauge line opened for freight traffic in 1859 and for passengers in 1883. Its passenger traffic finished in 1931 shortly after the line had been boughty by the Great Western Railway, who had a vested interest in the rival bus service, but its freight traffic lingered on until serious flooding in 1948 made the bridge over the river Dyfi to Machynlleth unsafe. A short section of track has been reopened near Corris and steam trains run along it on certain summer weekends. The line of the dismantled railway can be traced running parallel to the road on the far side.

Having come to this delightful valley, it would be a shame to miss its other attractions, notably the Corris Railway Museum and the Corris Craft Centre in Corris and the Centre for Alternative Technology between Corris and Machynlleth.

Refreshments   You'll have to bring your own picnic to this walk, but if you do combine it with a trip to the Corris Craft Centre, there is a cafe there (and shops in Corris). There is also an excellent wholefood,

continued on page 44

41

Route 9

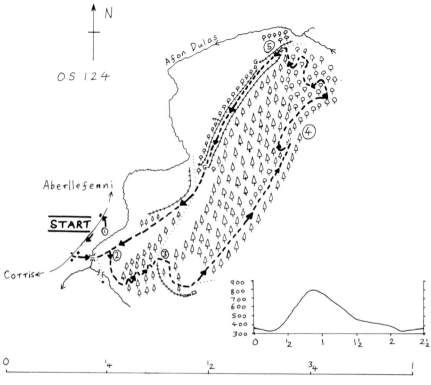

N

OS 124

Afon Dulas

⑤

④

Aberllefenni

START ①

② ③

Cottis←

900
800
700
600
500
400
300

0   ½   1   1½   2   2½

0   ¼   ½   ¾   1

The Cycle of Life
PEOPLE

FRESH VEGETABLES
FROM THE GARDEN
TO THE KITCHEN

THE ORGANIC GARDEN AT THE
CENTRE FOR ALTERNATIVE
TECHNOLOGY

Route 9

Foel Friog

2½ miles

START   *Look for a sign to the Forestry Commission's Foel Friog picnic place on your right as you drive along the lane between Corris and Aberllefenni. This is nearly two miles north-east of the A487 road at Corris. (G.R. SH769093)*

ROUTE

1. *Walk back to the lane from the picnic place and turn left along it towards Corris. Pass a building on your left and turn left along a track signed to Foel Friog Farm. Go across a bridge over the river and walk ahead along a clear track for 50 yards.*

2. *Turn right up a path which soon zig zags up through the trees. This route is waymarked with white footprints.*

3. *Fork right, uphill, and bear left after passing a ruin on your right. Go ahead along the waymarked forest path to a viewpoint.*

4. *Descend along the path from the viewpoint and follow a winding path down through trees to a lower path beside a fence.*

5. *Turn left through a gate and follow this clear, lower path back to the bridge over the river Dulas and retrace your steps to the start.*

Public Transport   The start of this walk is on the route of the No. 34 bus, which runs between Aberllefenni, Corris and Machynlleth at fairly regular intervals on weekdays. Consult the current bus timetable leaflet for Meirionnydd produced by Gwynedd County Council, or telephone Caernarfon 4121.

FOXGLOVE

Purple or cream. June - Sept.

vegetarian, cafe at the Centre for Alternative Technology. This place is ideal for children, with a maze and an adventure playground as well as the many interesting exhibits.

THE STANDING STONE AT CEFNCOCH-UCHAF

The Standing Stone at Cefncoch-uchaf

Outline Glantwymyn ~ Twymyn Valley path ~ Commins Coch ~ Woods ~ Standing Stone at Cefncoch-uchaf ~ Mountain views ~ Glantwymyn.

Summary Pleasant walking along a clear valley track parallel to the railway and river and partly shared with Glyndŵr's Way long-distance path (120 miles from Knighton to Welshpool via Machynlleth). A drop to cross the river at Commins Coch includes walking under the railway arches. A fairly stiff climb from Commins Coch to Cefncoch-uchaf is made into fun by having lots of yellow arrows to follow and stiles to climb, while the path encounters both evergreen and broadleaved trees. The standing-stone is at the highest point of the walk (700 ft.) and the view from here down to the bottom of the valley includes most of the mountains of southern Snowdonia, with Cadair Idris (2928 ft.) and Aran Fawddwy (2971 ft.) prominent. The paths are good underfoot and easy to follow.

Attractions This walk is both a haven of peace and tranquillity in easily accessible countryside and a safe, easily followed, exercise for young children who like to have something to spot in the distance. Glantwymyn (or Cemmaes Road) is a route centre, near the confluence of the river Dyfi with its tributary the Twymyn. The old Cambrian Railway Company connected Newtown and Machynlleth in 1863 and established a string of local halts along the line, including one at Cemmaes Road, so called because it served the ancient village of Cemmaes just 2 miles to the north. The railway remains popular today, with modern Sprinters and the diesel-hauled 'Cambrian Coast Express' rushing through the valley. They no longer stop at Cemmaes Road, however. The old station is 200 yards west of the roundabout on the Machynlleth Road and is now the bus stop. This used to be a junction, but the line from Cemmaes Road to Dinas Mawddwy, which opened in 1867, was finally closed in 1951. The main A470 road from north to south Wales can be seen across the valley and the environmental advantage of railway over road is made obvious, as is our mighty Victorian heritage with the triple-arched railway bridge over the Twymyn. Now, three long-distance paths meet in this valley, as ancient trackways must have done. These are the 274 mile Cambrian Way from Cardiff to Conwy, the 120 mile Glyndŵr's Way, from Knighton to

continued on page 48

Route 10

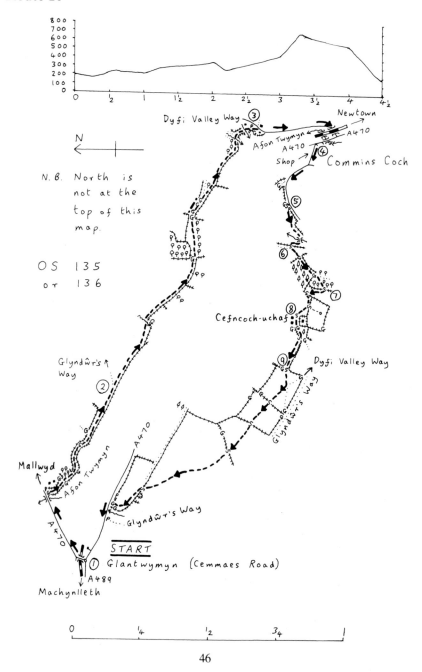

Dyfi Valley Way ③   Newtown

Afon Twymyn

A470

A470 ④ Commins Coch

Shop

N

N.B. North is
not at the
top of this
map.

OS 135
or 136

⑤

⑥

⑦

Cefncoch-uchaf ⑧

⑨   Dyfi Valley Way

Glyndŵr's
Way

②

Glyndŵr's Way

40

Mallwyd

Afon Twymyn

A470

Glyndŵr's Way

START
① Glantwymyn (Cemmaes Road)

A470

A489

Machynlleth

0   ¼   ½   ¾

Route 10

The Standing Stone at Cefncoch-uchaf   4½ miles

START   *Glantwymyn (or Cemmaes Road) is at the junction of the A470 and the A489, about 5 miles east of Machynlleth. Park in the little housing estate near Glantwymyn School, which is a left turn 100 yards east of the roundabout, in the direction of Newtown. (G.R. SH823044)*

ROUTE

1. *From the roundabout, cross the bridge over the railway in the direction of Dolgellau. Keep to the wide verge on the right. Cross a bridge over the river Twymyn and turn right along a signposted track. This is part of Glyndŵr's Way', which is followed to where it forks left uphill. Take the right fork and stay by the fence on your right in the valley.*

2. *Continue along this valley track, ignoring uphill forks on your left, until you meet a quiet back-road at a public footpath signpost.*

3. *Turn right down to Commins Coch, going under the railway arches and turning right along the A470 across the river Twymyn, for 200 yards.*

4. *Turn left towards the village telephone box and post office. Continue uphill and turn right at the T junction. Look for a signpost and waymarked stile beside a gate on your right.*

5. *Cross the stile and turn half-left down to a footbridge over a stream from where you bear right uphill to another waymarked stile.*

6. *Follow the path opposite uphill to a gate below evergreen trees on your left. Continue past these trees on your right to a second gate, then bear right uphill through broadleaved trees to a stile in the fence.*

7. *Turn half-right and walk up to a stile in the top fence. Continue to a stile in the fence on your left, giving access to the standing-stone.*

8. *Continue to the farm-buildings (Cefncoch-uchaf), where a step in a wooden fence gives access to the farm-yard. Follow the yellow arrows round to a stile in the fence on your right. Cross it and continue to another stile beside a gate in the corner of this field.*

9. *Follow the yellow arrows to cross three stiles in succession. Walk downhill to a stile giving access to a track where you turn left to reach the A470 at a signpost. Turn left along the road, ignoring the 'Glyndŵr's Way' signpost, back to the roundabout or your parked car.*

Public Transport Glantwymyn and Commins Coch are served by infrequent Crosville buses (S22) every weekday between Machynlleth and Newtown plus a bus on certain days only to Glantwymyn from Dinas Mawddwy (S18).

Welshpool via Machynlleth and the 108 mile Dyfi Valley Way from Aberdyfi to Borth via Aran Fawddwy. Don't be surprised to meet a weary backpacker or two!

Leys or earth-energy lines can be dowsed crossing at this standing-stone. It is interesting to note the possible directions of these lines. One ley could have gone past the site of the old hanging-tree on the slopes of Fron Goch, to the south-west, touched the western side of the earthwork on the summit of this possibly 'holy hill' and may even have extended to a cairn at G.R. SN764943. Notice that when looking down this line, the tip of the standing-stone resembles the silhouette of Fron Goch on the horizon, as illustrated in the photograph below.

Refreshments A shop is passed at Commins Coch (shut Thursday afternoons). There is a shop in Glantwymyn, opposite the bus stop.

THE RSPB'S VIEWPOINT ON FOEL FAWR.

48

Route 11
3 miles

Cwm Einion

Outline Furnace ~ Cwm Einion ~ Foel Fawr ~ Furnace.

Summary This is a splendid walk, featuring both the beautiful Cwm Einion, which is also known as 'Artist's Valley', and marvellous views over the Dyfi estuary, towards Aberdyfi. Just to add the icing to the cake, the restored charcoal-burning blast furnace near the finish of this walk makes an interesting visit and the leat or channel which provided water for its wheel can be followed to the top of a magnificent waterfall. If you want more, the entrance to the R.S.P.B.'s centre at Ynys-hir is near the start of the walk and you may be able to join a guided walk. The trees are at their best in the autumn.

Attractions Cwm Einion is not known as 'Artists' Valley' without good reason. The River Einion roars over the rocky bed of a deep gorge, which is clothed on its southern side with delightful woods. If you have the time, wander further up the valley to a lay-by and a Forestry Commission walk. This route takes you down to cross the river by a footbridge and to climb up the bare hillside opposite, although trees have now been planted in places here too.

Four hundred feet may not sound very high, but it looks like the top of a mountain from the clear path that leads around the bare side of Foel Fawr. The view well deserves the topograph placed along the path by the R.S.P.B. and overlooking their reserve at Ynys-hir. The Dyfi estuary rivals the Mawddach for scenic beauty, with the mountains of Meirionnydd providing a dramatic backcloth.

Furnace took its name from the ancient monument that has recently been restored and opened to the public. This was built about 1755 when the native deciduous forests of this area were valuable as providers of charcoal. This was used to make pig iron from iron ore brought from Cumbria, hence the importance of its coastal situation. A water wheel was necessary to power bellows which created a draught so that temperatures high enough to smelt iron could be attained. A leat or channel was constructed to feed this wheel with water. In order to have an adequate head of water, the river was dammed. This furnace was abandoned by 1810 and its present wheel dates from its later use as a sawmill. The spectacular waterfall remains, however.

Refreshments Hen Efail craft shop and restaurant is at the start of this walk. Children are welcome.

Route 11

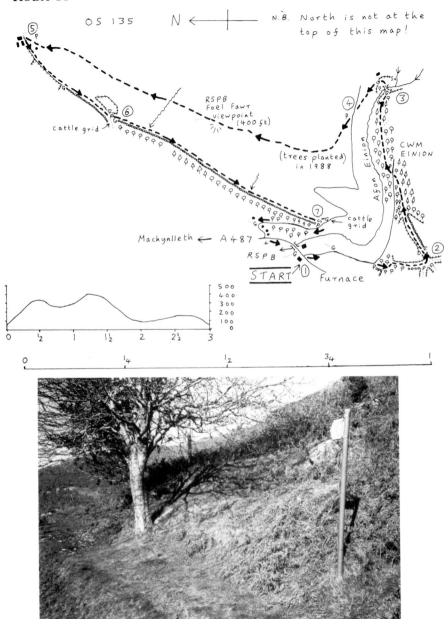

OS 135   N ⟵ ─┼─   N.B. North is not at the top of this map!

RSPB
Foel Fawr
viewpoint
(400 ft)

(trees planted)
in 1988

Afon Einion

CWM EINION

cattle grid

cattle grid

Machynlleth ⟵ A 487

RSPB

START Furnace

500
400
300
200
100
0

0   ½   1   1½   2   2½   3

0   ¼   ½   ¾   1

FOLLOW THIS SIGNPOSTED PATH ON THE CWM EINION WALK.

50

Route 11

Cwm Einion 3 miles

START *Furnace is on the A487 about five miles south-west of Machynlleth. There is a car park on your right as you come from Machynlleth, near the Hen Efail craft shop and restaurant. (G.R. SN684951)*

ROUTE

1. *From Hen Efail craft shop and restaurant, cross the A487 to go up the lane signposted Artists' Valley (Cwm Einion). Walk up this lane until it bends left. Leave it here, continuing up the signposted woodland path. Walk up to a crosstracks.*

2. *Turn left along the clear track. At first you have excellent, clear views across the Dyfi estuary on your left, then you descend through woodland. Cross the lane and go down the signposted path opposite. Descend through the trees to a footbridge across the river.*

3. *Cross the river and climb up the path which bends left and comes to another lane.*

4. *Cross the lane to a signposted footpath. This distinct path leads you around the hillside of Foel Fawr, passing the R.S.P.B.'s viewpoint on your left. Follow the clear, obvious path until it descends to a track near a farm.*

5. *Turn left along the farm access track, with a fence and then a wall on your right.*

6. *Turn left along a signposted path just before a cattle grid across the farm track. Walk with a wood behind the wall on your right.*

7. *Cross a stile on to a lane. Turn right down it to reach the A487 at Furnace. Turn left to cross the bridge (passing the waterfall on your left) and visit the blast furnace on your left before crossing the road to Hen Efail craft shop and restaurant and the car park.*

Public Transport Furnace has a regular weekday bus service, being on the route of Crosville's S14 bus which runs between Aberystwyth and Machynlleth. Telephone Aberystwyth 617951 for full details.

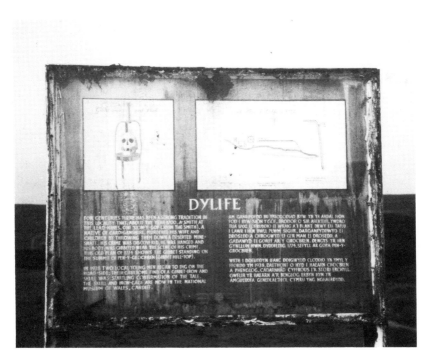

READ THIS NOTICE ABOUT SIÔN Y GOF WHERE 'GLYNDŴR'S WAY' MEETS
THE MOUNTAIN ROAD

Penycrocbren

Outline   Star Inn, Dylife ~ Glyndŵr's Way ~ Penycrocbren ~ Mountain Road ~ Starr Inn, Dylife.

Summary   An inspiring walk over windswept moorland. Mountain views can be enjoyed without the effort of climbing a mountain. Clear tracks are followed, so navigating is easy. Half of the route is part of the long distance route 'Glyndŵr's Way', which is waymarked. A small Roman fort is the chief feature of this high plateau, but it is a story of about 1700 which stirs the imagination. A mountain road leads back to Dylife, where the Star Inn survives as a reminder of the mining town that flourished here just over a century ago.

Attractions   Reserve this walk for a clear, sunny day, as the views add authenticity to the sense of remoteness and desolation in this part of Wales. If there's a bit of a breeze, it'll add to the atmosphere, but make sure you have enough warm clothes. These clear, wide, tracks are just the place to let go of the reins and feel free. If you look up into the sky, you may just see an expression of this —a Red Kite.

A notice at the start of this walk gives brief details of the old lead mines at Dylife. So famous were they that David Bick has devoted a book to their history. The Dylife mines revealed their full potential during the 19th century, but they may have been known to the Ancient Britons. The Romans may have built their fortlet beside the old road at Penycrocbren in order to protect these mines.

'Glyndŵr's Way' is a long distance walking route devised by Powys County Council. It is 120 miles long and leaves the Offa's Dyke Path at Knighton to head to Machynlleth, where Owain Glyndŵr was crowned as the last native, independent Prince of Wales in 1404, before representatives from France, Castile and Scotland. 'Glyndŵr's Way' then heads back to Offa's Dyke at Welshpool. It is up here, on these moorlands, that it seems closest to the spirit of the great Welsh patriot, who so nearly succeeded in forging an independent Welsh state. The scene of Glyndŵr's heroic victory at Hyddgen lies a few miles west of here. Dylife means 'place of floods' and is pronounced 'du-lee-ve'. It is coincidence that its name looks so appropriate in English, considering what happened here in about 1700. Penycrocbren is a name that does refer to this in Welsh, however, as it means 'Gallows-top'. The grim story is outlined on a second notice where 'Glyndŵr's Way' meets the

continued on page 56

Route 12

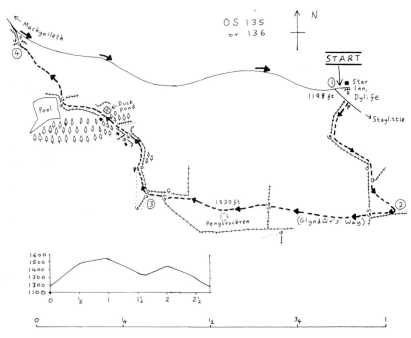

THE MID WALES REGIONAL OFFICE OF THE WALES TOURIST BOARD IS IN
THE OWAIN GLYNDŴR CENTRE, MACHYNLLETH

Route 12

Penycrocbren

2¾ miles

START   *Dylife is a remote place on the mountain road between Staylittle and Machynlleth, about two miles west of where it leaves the B4518 road north of Staylittle. Look for a telephone box and the Star Inn on your right as you come from Staylittle. There is plenty of space to park a car near the telephone box if you don't want to be a customer of the Star Inn. (GR. SN862940)*

ROUTE

1. *Cross the mountain road from the telephone box and turn left to a notice at the side of the road. This gives some information on the history of Dylife. The old lead mines were mostly on your right as you read this board. Go straight ahead along the signposted uphill track, away from the road, however. Keep the fence on your right until you go through a gate ahead, then bear left with the track to join the old road along the ridge which is part of the waymarked 'Glyndŵr's Way'.*

2. *Turn right along 'Glyndŵr's Way' along a track which was probably ancient in Roman times. Follow the waymarked route past the mounds of the Roman fortlet on your left and downhill beside a fence on your right.*

3. *Follow the waymarked route right along a track which bends left as it descends. Pass between conifer plantations, then pass a fenced duck pond on your right and a large pool where the infant Afon Twymyn was dammed to provide a reservoir of water for the lead mines on your left. Climb up to the mountain road where a 'Glyndŵr's Way' signpost keeps a notice about Siôn y Gof company.*

4. *Turn right along the mountain road, away from 'Glyndŵr's Way', to walk back to the telephone box and the Star Inn on your left.*

Public Transport   It could be said that Dylife is one of the most impractical places to reach by public transport. If you enjoy a real challenge, however, you could attempt it. There is a postal bus which leaves Llanidloes early in the morning, thus forcing you to spend the previous night near Llanidloes Post Office. Write to Llanidloes Post Office (Powys) for the current postal bus timetable. Alternatively, you could arrive in Dylife in the afternoon and spend the night at the Star Inn. Ramblers and even children are most welcome in this old inn, which has modern additions for a restaurant and bedrooms. Telephone the Star Inn on Llanbrynmair 345. The proprietors offer daily hacking from their own riding stables at special rates, while the food is home cooked.

mountain road. Incredibly, when you consider that overcrowding meant that the miners had to go to bed in shifts, Siôn y Gof (John the Smith) had a mistress in Dylife while he worked away from home. Perhaps he was surprised by a visit from his wife and daughter from Cwmystwyth, because he murdered them and threw their bodies down a mine shaft. Their bodies were discovered and Siôn, being the only blacksmith, had to make his own gibbet or iron cage in which his body was hung to rot.

Refreshments   The Star Inn, Dylife. Children welcome.

THE MONTGOMERYSHIRE CANAL NEAR THE START OF ROUTE 13.

Dolforwyn Castle

Outline   Lay-by on A483 ~ Montgomeryshire Canal Towpath ~ Aberbechan ~ Dolforwyn Castle ~ Lay-by on A483.

Summary   Navigation is no problem on this walk. After following the canal towpath, you take to country lanes, with the exception of a brief diversion to visit Dolforwyn Castle. The climb up to the ruins of the castle is also the only strenuous part of this walk, but the magnificent view is well worth it.

Attractions   The Montgomeryshire Canal was dug to link the rivers Mersey and Severn. It became a great local asset, bringing lime to spread on the acid soils of the Severn Valley that had been used for rough grazing until the Industrial Revolution brought both the means to improve the land and the market to sell the produce. This therefore became an agricultural canal, rather than a route between Liverpool and Bristol. The decision to extend the canal from Welshpool to Newtown (then known as 'The Leeds of Wales') was made in 1794, but its final section was not opened until 1821. The railways were soon to provide competition, but the canal functioned well into the 20th century, being officially abandoned in 1944. Although neglected, the canal is now being revived by the enthusiasts who restore it for recreation. A practical way to use it is by canoe, where you are almost at eye level with the swans, moorhens and, if you are lucky, kingfishers that thrive in this habitat. For walkers, the canal towpath provides easy access to the beautiful Montgomeryshire countryside.

The scenery changes dramatically at Dolforwyn Castle. From a gentle, sluggish, valley, you are at the top of a hill with inspiring views. The Severn Valley unfolds below you and it was the strategic aspect of this point that led Llywelyn ap Gruffydd (Llywelyn the Last) to build a castle here in 1273. Being a native Welsh castle, it is comparatively small, but some imposing fragments remain. In its short history, Dolforwyn Castle honourably met an attempt by the Norman constable of Montgomery to take it, with the Welsh triumphing at 'the Massacre of Abermiwl Barn'. According to ancient legend the British princess Habren (Sabrina) was drowned near Dolforwyn, and gave her name to the river Severn.

Refreshments   There are none available on the walk, but there is a shop in the village of Abermule.

Route 13

OS 136

Welshpool

START→
(at lay-by)

Dolforwyn
Castle

Yew Tree
Cottage

6

5

hut

A483

B4386

Canal
Tunnel

Lock G

Abermule
(D75 Bus
& shop)

Lock G

Newtown

Montgomeryshire Canal

River Severn
(Afon Hafren)

B4568

4

B4389

Aberbechan

3

800
700
600
500
400
300
200

0   ½   1   1½   2   2½   3   3½   4   4½

0   ¼   ½   ¾   1

MOORHEN   Black, white, red beak. 33cm.

58

Route 13
Dolforwyn Castle

4¾ miles

START *Look for a lay-by on your right as you drive north-eastwards along the A483 from Newtown, by-passing Abermule by crossing the river Severn by the new road bridge. The lay-by is immediately after the next turning on your right, which also leads to Abermule, but by an old road bridge over the canal. (G.R. SO162952)*

ROUTE

1. *Facing the direction of Newtown (south-west), turn left off the A483 to cross the old canal bridge. Your way is through a gate on your right to reach a stile which gives access to the canal towpath. First, however, inspect the bridge ahead that spans the river Severn. This was the second iron bridge to be built in Montgomeryshire.*

2. *Walk along the towpath with the canal on your right. When the canal goes through a tunnel under the new road bridge, follow the fence on your left. Go under the new road and across a stile beside a gate to regain the canal towpath after crossing another stile. Continue along the towpath until a scrapyard on your left heralds the old canal community of Aberbechan.*

3. *Cross a stile on to a lane, but don't continue over the next stile back to the towpath. This is Aberbechan, where you turn right over the canal and up the lane to join the B4389 road.*

4. *Take the first turning on your right to follow a delightful lane. Go right when you come to a fork and bend sharply right to contour around a hill with woodland on your left. Watch out for a sign to 'Yew Tree Cottage' just after a hut on your left.*

5. *Turn left through a gate and up an access track to Yew Tree Cottage. Pass the cottage on your right as you go through a gate ahead. Turn right uphill to find the ruins of Dolforwyn Castle at the summit.*

6. *Retrace your steps to the lane. Turn left to continue in the same direction as before. Ignore a turning on your right. Descend to a junction and turn right to reach the A483, where the lay-by is across the road on your right.*

   (If you can manage another quarter of a mile, go back to where you first joined the canal towpath, but go right this time, under the old road bridge and with the canal on your left. You soon reach a fine example of the restoration work being done on this canal, to locks, bridges, warehouses and cottages. Retrace your steps to the lay-by.)

Public Transport At one time, trains stopped at Abermule. Now the Sprinters of British Rail's Shrewsbury - Machynlleth line flash past parallel to the river Severn and the Montgomeryshire Canal. The A483 shares this same transport corridor and Crosville's D75 bus runs along it regularly between Newtown and Welshpool (tel. Oswestry 652402 for full details). Bus passengers will have to alight in the village of Abermule and walk north-eastwards along the B4386 until a turning on your left leads to the bridges over the river Severn and the canal.

ABERYSTWYTH HARBOUR

Pen Dinas

Outline   Aberystwyth ~ Harbour ~ Monument ~ Aberystwyth.

Summary   Most visitors see the modern seaside resort of Aberystwyth, with its pebbly beach stretching from the pier to Constitution Hill, with its Cliff Railway and Camera Obscura. This walk explores the old Aberystwyth, however, where you'll be away from the crowds and won't be tempted to spend money. This is the real Aberystwyth, as it does actually overlook the river Ystwyth. The modern town should really be renamed Aber-rheidol, meaning the mouth of the Rheidol. Starting from Aberystwyth Railway Station, this walk goes across the Trefechan Bridge, over the river Rheidol and past Aberystwyth harbour, with its yachts. A good path gradually climbs up to the 415 foot summit of Pen Dinas, with its Wellington monument. You descend on the other side of this old hillfort to return to Aberystwyth.

Attractions   The walk emphasises the age of the place we still know as Aberystwyth. Pen Dinas is an iron age hillfort, dating from about 300 B.C. This was a long time after the stone age people who established a flint factory near the base of Pen Dinas in about 400 B.C. The strange monument on the top of Pen Dinas is almost modern, however. It is shaped like a cannon barrel and was erected in 1852 in memory of the Duke of Wellington, victor of Waterloo. It was intended to erect a statue of the duke on horseback on top of the monument, but the funds didn't run to this. Despite the monument's similarity to a factory chimney, it does have a certain charm and the view is superb, overlooking Cardigan Bay to the west.

   Aberystwyth has a fine natural harbour. This fact led to the Normans building a castle here in 1277. Such a construction job was made possible in the heart of Welsh Wales because materials and labour could be brought by sea. The port was also used to land vast quantities of herring. One and a quarter million herring were landed in one night in 1745 by 47 boats working from Aberystwyth. As ships grew in size, however, they found it harder to negotiate the sand and shingle bar at the harbour mouth. The stone quays built in the early 19th century enabled trade to continue, however. Agricultural produce was exported and coal landed to fuel the lime kilns. Ships were built here until 1880, but the harbour is now devoted to pleasure craft.

Refreshments   There are plenty of places to choose from in Aberystwyth.

Route 14

N

OS 135

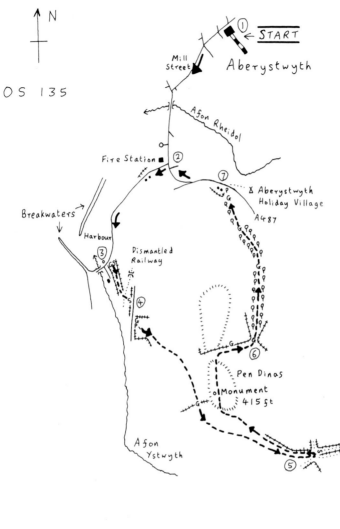

Aberystwyth

START

Mill Street

Afon Rheidol

Fire Station ② ⑦

Breakwaters

Harbour

Dismantled Railway

③

④

⑥

⑤

Aberystwyth Holiday Village

A487

Pen Dinas
Monument
415 ft

Afon Ystwyth

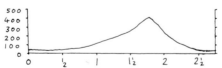

500
400
300
200
100
0

0   ½   1   1½   2   2½

0   ¼   ½   ¾   1

Route 14
Pen Dinas

2¾ miles

START *Aberystwyth can be reached by train or bus, while there are signposted car parks. Start from the railway station, which serves as the terminus for the Vale of Rheidol narrow gauge line as well as the line to Shrewsbury. (G.R. SN585816)*

ROUTE

1. *With your back to the railway station, turn left and go ahead down Mill Street to cross the bridge over the river Rheidol.*

2. *Turn right just after the Fire Station and follow a lane to the harbour, which is on your right.*

3. *Just before a pill-box which guarded the harbour on your right and a bridge over the river Ystwyth ahead, turn left over a stile beside a gate. Go ahead to cross the trackbed of the now dismantled railway which went from Aberystwyth to Carmarthen and reach a lane.*

4. *Go right along the lane until a signposted path on the left leads uphill through a gate. Follow this well-defined path as it makes a gradual ascent of Pen Dinas.*

5. *When you reach a crosstracks with a stile ahead of you, double back to the left and follow a narrow path slightly higher than the one you came here by. Walk with a fence on your right, then continue up to the monument at the summit. Go straight on down to another fence and turn right. Pass a gate on your left and go to a second gate in the corner of the field ahead on your left.*

6. *Go through the gate and down a tree-lined path. Continue until a gate leads to the A487 road at a public footpath signpost.*

7. *Turn left to follow the A487 back to the start of the walk.*

Public Transport Aberystwyth is at the end of the British Rail line from Shrewsbury. There are through trains from and to Birmingham and London. There are also several buses which can bring you here and they stop just outside the railway station. The best way to come here is by steam train from Devil's Bridge.

CROSS THE RIVER RHEIDOL BY THIS FOOTBRIDGE. THE "STAG" CAN BE
SEEN ON THE HILL BEYOND.

Cwm Rheidol

Outline   Lakeside Picnic Site ~ Dam ~ Nature Trail ~ Rheidol Falls ~
Rheidol Power Station ~ Reception Centre ~ Lakeside Picnic Site.

Summary   Easy, pleasant walking beside a reservoir created in the
Rheidol Valley to regulate the flow of the river below the hydro-
electricity scheme. Half of the walk is along a lane, while the other half is
along a woodland path which descends to the river bank before crossing a
footbridge near a waterfall and fish ladder.

Attractions   This walk is set in a beautifully wooded valley which has not
suffered from the creation of a reservoir associated with the Rheidol
Power Station. May would be a good time to come and see the bluebells in
the woods, but the autumn is the best time to enjoy the colour of the
native, broad-leaved trees. If you come on a summer evening, you can see
the dam floodlit between 9 p.m. and 11 p.m. but then you'd be too late to
visit the hydro-electric power station, which is open from 11 a.m. to 4.30
p.m. between Easter and September (from 12 noon to 4 p.m. in
October). Tickets for this tour can be purchased at the Reception Centre,
which houses an exhibition on the hydro-electric scheme and the history
of electricity.

Whenever you come, the 'stag' will be on the hillside to the north to
greet you. This shape was formed naturally when waste spoil from old
lead and zinc mines above was dumped over the side of the valley. The
scree is too poisonous to sustain vegetation. The best view of the 'stag' is
from the 'Lein Fach', the steam railway which climbs the opposite side of
the valley and provides an enjoyable means of transport to this walk from
either Aberystwyth or Devil's Bridge.

The dam contains a small, auxiliary power station, but it is the solid,
square building fed by two great pipes from above (bringing water under
great pressure from the Dinas Reservoir higher up) near the eastern end
of this walk that contains the dynamos which send 40,000 kilowatts of
electricity into the national grid. Both ends of this lake (it's too pretty to
be termed a reservoir) have ways of helping trout and salmon upstream to
spawn in the gravels of the river bed. The dam contains a fish lift, while a
fish ladder avoids the high waterfall upstream. You can divert upstream a
few yards before crossing the footbridge just below the waterfall.

Refreshments   The Tea Gardens on your right shortly after the Power
Station sell ice-creams to passers-by, while refreshments are also

continued on page 68

65

Route 15

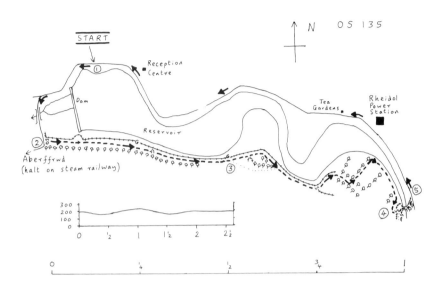

ANOTHER VIEW OF THE "STAG" ACROSS THE RESERVOIR.

Route 15
Cwm Rheidol

2½ miles

START *The Cwm Rheidol Reservoir is about 8 miles east of Aberystwyth, from where it can be reached by road along either the A44 (turning right as signposted at Capel Bangor) or the A4120 (forking left down to Aberffrwd). Park in the lay-by of the picnic area on your right just after the dam. A good idea in the summer would be to take the steam train from either Aberystwyth or Devil's Bridge and alight at the halt at Aberffrwd. If you do this, turn left down the road into Aberffrwd. Turn sharp right at the road junction in the village and follow this road towards the Cwm Rheidol Dam. Don't bend left with the road to cross the Felin Newydd bridge to meet the main valley road, as you can start this walk from point 2, a gate on the right at the bend in the road. The walk from and to Aberffrwd halt adds 1½ miles to the length of this walk. (G.R. SN695796, re. the car park start at point 1).*

ROUTE

1. With your back to the reservoir and picnic site, turn left along the road. Turn left at the road junction to cross the bridge over the river Rheidol, with a fine view of the dam on your left.

2. Turn left through the gate, or over the stile beside it, at the bend in the road. A sign marks this as the start of the C.E.G.B. Nature Trail. Follow the broad, clear path with the reservoir on your left.

3. When the path forks, go left (but not down through the gate). Keep to the top of a steep slope above the reservoir. Go through a gate ahead to descend on your left to a tree-lined path. Just after the second row of trees running across the meadow to the river, turn left and walk towards the power station, then turn right to walk along the river bank upstream.

4. Cross the stile in the fence on your left which gives access to a path down to the footbridge. Pause awhile at this delightful spot, however. A stile opposite leads into another picnic site, while the path on the right brings you to a view of the fish ladder which avoids the high waterfall. Eventually, cross the footbridge and walk up to the road.

5. Turn left along the road. Pass the Rheidol Power Station on your right, followed by Tea Gardens which offer ice-creams for sale to passers-by. More road-walking, with the reservoir on your left, brings you to the Reception Centre (where there are toilets) on your right before the lay-by and picnic site where you started on your left.

Public Transport The best way is to travel to the halt at Aberffrwd on the narrow gauge steam-hauled Vale of Rheidol Railway, which runs between Aberystwyth and Devil's Bridge. If you come out of season, however, when the trains may not be running, there are still buses from Aberystwyth to Capel Bangor, but this adds an extra 3 miles of road walking each way. If you don't mind this, telephone Aberystwyth 617951 (Crosville) or 611085 (Roberts Coaches) for the times of service no. 501.

---

available in the Reception Centre. There are picnic sites at the start (and finish) of the walk and at the half-way point.

PENYGARREG DAM

Route 16

Penygarreg Reservoir

Outline   Penbont Car Park ~ Elan Valley Railway ~ Craig Goch Dam ~ Penygarreg Dam ~ Penbont Car Park.

Summary   Once you have made the ascent from the car park to the line of the dismantled railway, this is a level walk, until the final descent. Navigation is made easy by the width of the track and the fact that you keep to the side of the lake (it's too attractive to be called a reservoir). The return half of this walk is along a road, in order to allow you to complete the circle around the lake. Traffic is light and confined to the tourist season, but if you prefer to keep your peace of mind, simply retrace your steps along the old railway line when you reach the dam of Craig Goch Reservoir (stage 4).

Attractions   You can't visit Mid Wales without seeing Wales' very own Lake District — the Elan Valley. this beauty is artificial, but the engineering feats merely serve to enhance the fact that the scenery here is magnificent. The dams across the Elan Valley were built by Birmingham Corporation around 1900. The manufacturing heart of the British Empire had outgrown its water supply and needed to import water from Wales. Apart from the creation of reservoirs on the river Elan and the river Claerwen, an aqueduct was built to carry the water the 73 miles to Birmingham. Since the water left here at a height of 770 feet and Birmingham is 600 feet above sea level, there was a fall of only 170 feet over those 73 miles. The engineers therefore had to construct an aqueduct with an average gradient of only 1 in 2300. Over 75 million gallons of water a day flow along it.

In order to construct the dams, a railway had to be built to carry the stones and other materials. This was an impressive feat of engineering in itself, as is evident when you walk part of its trackbed. This seven mile railway was opened in 1894 and closed in 1917. It connected with the Mid Wales Railway just south of Rhayader.

A feature of the walk along the old railway is the oak woodland, which harbours a wide variety of wildlife, including small birds such as Blue Tits, Great Tits and Goldcrests. Look out too for the rare Red Kite.

Refreshments   Bring your own!

Route 16

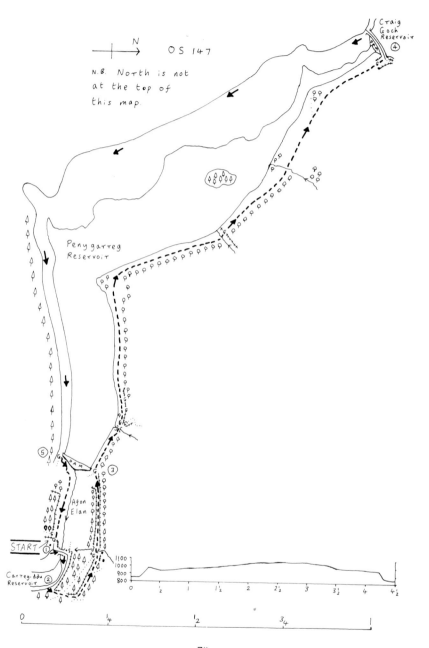

N
OS 147

N.B. North is not
at the top of
this map.

Craig
Goch
Reservoir
④

Peny garreg
Reservoir

⑤

DAM

③

Afon
Elan

START ①

Carreg-ddu ②
Reservoir

1100
1000
900
800

0   ½   1   1½   2   2½   3   3½   4   4½

0   ¼   ½   ¾   1

70

Route 16
Penygarreg Reservoir

4½ miles

START   *Penbont Car Park is four miles from the Elan Valley Visitor Centre, which is at the end of the B4518. This is four miles south-west of Rhayader, where the A44 meets the A470. Continue along the minor road from the Elan Valley Visitor Centre towards the Penygarreg Dam. The car park is on your right just after crossing the bridge over the river Elan. (G.R. SN914673)*

ROUTE

1. *Walk back to the road and turn left across the bridge over the river Elan. The Penygarreg Dam is on your left. Follow the road as it bends right, passing a telephone box and with a fence on your left, behind which are conifer trees.*

2. *When the fence on your left ends, turn left along a steep uphill path through the trees. There is a fence on your left at first, then a gap where you cross the old trackbed of the Elan Valley Railway before the fence resumes on your left and stays with you until you reach a forest road above the trees. Turn left along this forest road until you are level with the top of Penygarreg Dam on your left.*

3. *Go through a gate ahead to walk along the trackbed of the dismantled railway with the reservoir on your left. Continue along this clear, wide, track until the Craig Goch Dam.*

4. *If you are not going to retrace your steps from here, turn left along the road across the top of Craig Goch Dam and turn left to follow the road which overlooks the Penygarreg Reservoir on your left. Follow this road until you are level with the top of the Penygarreg Dam on your left.*

5. *Turn left through a gate and go down a path to the foot of the dam. Turn right to walk with the river Elan on your left back to the car park at Penbont.*

Public Transport   None.

A TRAIN FROM PORTHMADOG ENTERING TAN-Y-BWLCH STATION (ROUTE 1). NOTICE THE MINIATURE RAILWAY TRACK ON THE LEFT.

Appendices

Approximate mileage of each Walk from Machynlleth via main roads.

Route	Machynlleth
1	33
2	22
3	37
4	35
5	13
6	12
7	18
8	9
9	5
10	5
11	5
12	8
13	30
14	16
15	23
16	35

ROUTES IN ORDER OF DIFFICULTY

None of these walks would be strenuous to an experienced walker. The following grading is made in the context of a Family Walks book and is done with the fairly active six or seven year old in mind.

Easy Walks

Route 2 — *Maesgwm*
Route 3 — *Pennant-Melangell*
Route 4 — *Llangynog*
Route 5 — *Plas yn Dinas*
Route 15 — *Cwm Rheidol*

Moderately difficult

Route 1 — *Tan-y-bwlch*
Route 6 — *Meirion Mill*
Route 11 — *Cwm Einion*
Route 13 — *Dolforwyn Castle*
Route 14 — *Pen Dinas*
Route 16 — *Penygarreg Reservoir*

More Strenuous

Route 7 — *Garthbeibio*
Route 8 — *Abergynolwyn*
Route 9 — *Foel Friog*
Route 10 — *The Standing Stone at Cefncoch-uchaf*
Route 12 — *Penycrocbren*

A RESTORED SECTION OF THE MONTGOMERYSHIRE CANAL,
NEAR DOLFORWYN CASTLE (ROUTE 13).

PUBLIC TRANSPORT

Public transport is sparse in Mid Wales, but it is enjoyable and deserving of support. British Rail have three lines, from Shrewsbury to Aberystwyth, from Machynlleth to Pwllheli and from Shrewsbury to Swansea via Llandrindod. There are also the 'great little trains of Wales', which are listed in the wet weather alternatives. A leaflet giving details of them all is available from the Wales Tourist Board. Buses vary from county to county. Gwynedd, which includes Meirionnydd, is best, with a common rover ticket and comprehensive timetables and maps. Send a 9" x 6" s.a.e. to the County Planning Department, County Council Offices, Caernarfon, Gwynedd, LL55 1SH, or tel. 0286 4121. Dyfed, which includes Ceredigion, is satisfactory, producing a map and list of operators. Send a 9" x 6" s.a.e. to Dyfed County Council, Highways and Transportation Dept., Llanstephan Road, Carmarthen, SA31 3LZ, or tel. 0267 233333. Powys, which includes Montgomeryshire and Radnorshire, is poor. Tel. 0597 3711. One of the biggest bus companies in Mid Wales is Crosville Cymru. Tel. 0970 617951.

74

Wales Tourist Board, Mid Wales Regional Office, Canolfan Owain Glyndŵr, Machynlleth, Powys, SY20 8EE, tel. 0654 2401.

There are Tourist Information Centres at Aberdyfi, Aberystwyth, Bala, Barmouth, Blaenau Ffestiniog, Corris, Dolgellau, Elan Valley, Harlech, Llandrindod Wells, Llanidloes, Llanfyllin, Newtown, Rhayader, Tywyn and Welshpool.

THE HOLLOW OAK TREE NEAR FOEL-LŴYD (ROUTE 7).

WET WEATHER ALTERNATIVES. Completely or partly under cover.

It does rain in Wales, so it is useful to know where to go if it's too wet for a walk. The following list is not comprehensive and current tourist information should be consulted. It is arranged by its proximity to each walk.

Walk 1: *Portmeirion Italianate Village, Harlech Castle, Llechwedd Slate Caverns, Gloddfa Ganol Slate Mine, Ffestiniog Railway, Welsh Highland Railway, C.E.G.B. Ffestiniog Pumped Storage Scheme, Porthmadog Pottery and Old Llanfair Slate Caverns.*

Walk 2: *Penmaenpool Nature Information Centre; Old Country Life Museum, Talybont; R.N.L.I. Museum, Barmouth; Maes Artro Tourist Village, Llanbedr.*

Walks 3 & 4: *Bala Lake Railway; Lake Vyrnwy Visitor Centre; Cyffdy Farm Park, Llanuwchllyn.*

Walks 5 & 6: *Meirion Mill.*

Walk 7: *Welshpool and Llanfair Light Railway.*

Walk 8: *Talyllyn Railway and Museum; Holgates Honey Farm, Tywyn; Tywyn Swimming Pool; Fairbourne Railway and Butterfly Safari; Aberdyfi Maritime Museum; Tywyn Cinema.*

Walk 9: *Corris Craft Centre, Corris Railway and Museum, Centre for Alternative Technology.*

Walk 10: *Owain Glyndŵr Exhibition, Machynlleth; Felin Crewi.*

Walk 11: *Dyfi Furnace; R.S.P.B. Ynyshir; Old Chapel Museum, Tre'r Ddol.*

Walk 12: *Llanidloes Museum.*

Walk 13: *Welshpool and Llanfair Light Railway; Powis Castle and Clive Museum; Montgomery Canal Boat Trips; Powysland Museum; Montgomery Castle; Robert Owen Museum, Newtown; W. H. Smith Museum, Newtown.*

Walk 14: *Aberystwyth Swimming Pool, Aberystwyth Arts Centre, Aberystwyth Cliff Railway, Camera Obscura, Ceredigion Museum, Vale of Rheidol Railway, Glan y Mor Leisure Park, Aberystwyth Cinema.*

Walk 15: *Vale of Rheidol Railway, Llywernog Silver-Lead Mine, C.E.G.B. Rheidol Hydro-Electric Scheme.*

Walk 16: *Elan Valley Visitor Centre; Cambrian Factory, Llanwrtyd Wells; Llandrindod Wells Museum; Llandrindod Wells Swimming Pool.*

A WINDMILL AT THE CENTRE FOR ALTERNATIVE TECHNOLOGY NEAR
MACHYNLLETH AND NEAR ROUTE 9

FAMILY WALKS SERIES

Family Walks in the North Yorkshire Dales. Howard Beck. ISBN 0 907758 52 5.

Family Walks in West Yorkshire. Howard Beck. ISBN 0 907758 43 6.

Family Walks in Three Peaks and Malham. Howard Beck. ISBN 0 907758 42 8.

Family Walks in South Yorkshire. Norman Taylor. ISBN 0 907758 25 8.

Family Walks in the North Wales Borderlands. Gordon Emery. ISBN 0 907758 50 9.

Family Walks in Cheshire. Chris Buckland. ISBN 0 907758 29 0.

Family Walks in the Staffordshire Peak and Potteries. Les Lumsdon. ISBN 0 907758 34 7.

Family Walks in the White Peak. Norman Taylor. ISBN 0 907758 09 6.

Family Walks in the Dark Peak. Norman Taylor. ISBN 0 907758 16 9.

Family Walks in Snowdonia. Laurence Main. ISBN 0 907758 32 0.

Family Walks in Mid Wales. Laurence Main. ISBN 0 907758 27 4.

Family Walks in South Shropshire. Marian Newton. ISBN 0 907758 30 4.

Family Walks in the Teme Valley. Camilla Harrison. ISBN 0 907758 45 2.

Family Walks in Hereford and Worcester. Gordon Ottewell. ISBN 0 907758 20 7.

Family Walks around Cardiff and the Valleys. Gordon Hindess. ISBN 0 907758 54 1.

Family Walks in the Wye Valley. Heather and Jon Hurley. ISBN 0 907758 26 6.

Family Walks around Stratford and Banbury. Gordon Ottewell. ISBN 0 907758 49 5.

Family Walks in the Cotswolds. Gordon Ottewell. ISBN 0 907758 15 0.

Family Walks in South Gloucestershire. Gordon Ottewell. ISBN 0 907758 33 9.

Family Walks in Oxfordshire. Laurence Main. ISBN 0 907758 38 X.

Family Walks around Bristol, Bath and the Mendips. Nigel Vile. ISBN 0 907758 19 3.

Family Walks in Wiltshire. Nigel Vile. ISBN 0 907758 21 5.

Family Walks in Berkshire and North Hampshire. Kathy Sharp. ISBN 0 907758 37 1.

Family Walks on Exmoor and the Quantocks. John Caswell. ISBN 0 907758 46 0.

Family Walks in Mendip, Avalon and Sedgemoor. Nigel Vile. ISBN 0 907758 41 X.

Family Walks in Cornwall. John Caswell. ISBN 0 907758 55 X.

Family Walks on the Isle of Wight. Laurence Main. ISBN 0 907758 56 8.

Family Walks in North West Kent. Clive Cutter. ISBN 0 907758 36 3.

Family Walks in the Weald of Kent and Sussex. Clive and Sally Cutter. ISBN 0 907758 51 7.

The Publishers, D. J. Mitchell and E. G. Power welcome suggestions for further titles in this Series; and will be pleased to consider manuscripts relating to Derbyshire from new or established authors.

Scarthin Books of Cromford are the leading Peak District specialists in secondhand and antiquarian books, and purchase good books, music, maps and photographs at fair and informed valuations.

Contact Dr. D. J. Mitchell by letter, or phone Matlock (0629) 823272.